Concerto al-Quds

Adonis
Concerto al-Quds

أدونيس
كونشيرتو القدس

TRANSLATED FROM THE ARABIC BY

KHALED MATTAWA

YALE UNIVERSITY PRESS ■ NEW HAVEN & LONDON

A MARGELLOS
WORLD REPUBLIC OF LETTERS BOOK

The Margellos World Republic of
Letters is dedicated to making literary
works from around the globe available
in English through translation. It brings
to the English-speaking world the work
of leading poets, novelists, essayists,
philosophers, and playwrights from
Europe, Latin America, Africa, Asia, and
the Middle East to stimulate international
discourse and creative exchange.

Yale University Press books may be purchased
in quantity for educational, business, or
promotional use. For information, please e-mail
sales.press@yale.edu (U.S. office) or sales@
yaleup.co.uk (U.K. office).

Set in Electra and Nobel type by Tseng
Information Systems, Inc.
Printed in the United States of America.

Library of Congress Control Number:
2017941088
ISBN 978-0-300-19764-8 (hardcover : alk. paper)

A catalogue record for this book is available from
the British Library.
This paper meets the requirements of ANSI/
NISO Z39.48-1992 (Permanence of Paper).

10 9 8 7 6 5 4 3 2 1

Al-Quds (القدس) is the Arabic name for Jerusalem.

Bait al-Maqdis (بيت المقدس) is the part of the city of al-Quds that contains

the al-Aqsa mosque (المسجد الأقصى), al-Masjid al-Aqsa,

as well as Qibbat al-Sakhra (قبة الصخرة), which is known as the Dome of the Rock.

CONTENTS

Concerto al-Quds

PART I *The Meaning*

1. HEAVENLY SUMMARY

Up there, up above,
look at her dangling from the sky's throat.
Look at her fenced with the eyelashes of angels.

No one can walk toward her,
but a man can crawl on his forehead and shoulders,
                    perhaps even his navel.

Barefoot, knock on her door.
A prophet will open, and teach you how to march, and how to bow.

A stage play directed by the all-wise, the almighty.
And the Lord does this for the sake of all his children:

"Here I am, a silhouette of al-Quds,"
cried a three-headed dummy on the stage, then exited.

"Bait al-Maqdis,[1] fearing ruin, complained to the Lord and the Lord revealed to it,
'I will fill you with prostrate faces that long for you
the way doves long for their eggs.'"

"Fear God, O Ka'b!
          Does al-Quds have a tongue?"

"Yes, and a heart like you."[2]

A stage play directed by the all-wise, the almighty.

❀

Many times I begged bread to criticize salt.
Many times someone whispered to me,
                              "Why is death always late in al-Quds,
        while the march of life becomes another death?"
And how can a head be imprisoned
                    in a cellar of words it had invented?

Truly, the Unknown becomes deceptive in al-Quds,
          and he is the master of all deceivers.[3]

In a corner, in the farthest reaches of my desert,
a gazelle weeps.

❀

Time rushing through the streets of al-Quds,
                          I know your name.
I was commanded to offer you uranium extract.
                          I will command the moon
to sign your notebook,
              and the sun to date the signing.
And look at these walls spilling the milk of their sadness on the earth, celebrating you.

And Time, as you know,
the ants stand higher in God's eyes than all the planets:
They spoke to Solomon,
but the planets never could.[4]
Perhaps this is why ants can prophesy:

(Belts. Masks. Trenches. Earthmovers. Bombs. Missiles. Suitcases. Tires. Artificial
Intelligence.)

These are the coming days.

That is why the sky becomes
a secret hole in history's ceiling.

"Bait al-Maqdis, land of summoning and resurrection."[5]
"Whoever dies in Bait al-Maqdis is like one who dies in the heavens."[6]

But here's Imru-ulqais passing
through on his way to Byzantium![7]
Before his feet touch the threshold of Bait al-Maqdis, he reads,
The blood shed on Mediterranean shores,
since its beginnings, has spelled a ravaged history.
And the earth's history
has a heavenly summary named al-Quds.

But why do only two kinds of people live here:
the dead who inhabit the desert
and the living who reside in graves?

Day and night wrestle
to choke one another in the name of al-Quds.
Time was busy filming the battle, turning it into a documentary.
Leaving the scene, Imru-ulqais says,
"In the beginning was the word.
In the beginning of the word was 'blood.'"

A stage play directed by the all-wise, the almighty.

Imru-ulqais, aren't you tired of walking these streets paved by the Unknown?
How excellent they are at tracking you, these roads!
How powerful their walls at intercepting people's words!
Every time you try to embrace a woman, a guard asks you,
        "Do you have the heavens' permission?"

Indeed, all the fruit of these streets is bitter.
Still you go on walking, more persistently than a hungry male ant, making of your
steps chords for music that has not been composed,
    encircled by dream-blown flutes
                whose masculinity drives away the eggs of doubt.

You doubt if your bed is another night altogether.
Something whispers to you,
"Night lies, as usual, even though
            he is the sun's most loyal friend."
But you know by now how to start from point zero,
            having smelled so often the scent of eternities.
Your grandmother, that 'Ukazi sky,[8] slipped coins into her sons' pockets
            which were actually dice.

She commanded they throw them on the sands of the stars if they wanted to dissolve in their dreams.

Obeying her commands,
they cast their odes on the sand
in blessing and celebration.

You are under another sky now. Bleeding walls surround you. Heads that are almost severed speak without cease.

Have no fear, dear Wind.

The traps you have set hide forests of fire behind them.

And there are blood gushers dripping from the eye of the needle the sky holds in her hand.

Words, swords, and spears
prey on anyone who can discern.

—Angels prefer to make love, and that the smoke of Arab musk shelter them in their banishment between Hijaz and al-Quds.[9]

Your sky is a semantic etching. Your earth pushes a carriage of delusions. Whenever a word heaves among the etchings,

the teeth of history chatter, and heads roll like balls in all directions while the stars squat like bundles of straw.

—A history, a milk that flees our mothers' breasts to feed the moon and the rest of the planets.

—When the storm assaults, it uses only our bodies as weapons.

It fills our days
with black clouds that even light cannot read.

—This way we will continue making coffins before their time is due. We anoint them with the perfume of pre-creation. And in their names we slit
the earth's arteries to feed the veins of the Unknown.

—Read your horoscope, dear History, and you will see how delusions turn into towers of facts.

—The body of history surrenders on astrology's bed.
Here it is
unbuttoning its clothes.

❀

The wind reads the roses.
Perfume writes them.

A woman in love enters her garden in al-Quds where her love resides.
The flowers become nets that encircle her steps.
She laughs and says,
        "Must I sew a new dress for every flower here?"
Yesterday when I met her, night whispered in my ear,
        "Perfume is the rose's child,
        but he is born a young man."

(Tension. Homicide. Arrest. Ambulances. Fire engines. Victims. Accusations.
Prohibitions. Insurrection. Infiltration. Interrogation. Detention units. Apprehension.
        Prisons. Demolition. Occupation.)

I said to my imagination, "Be brave,
        and put your hands on the shoulders of al-Quds."
And I said to al-Quds,
        "Why is it that when I come toward you, I can only walk backward?"

(Terrorism. Kidnapping. Unknown entity. Extremism. Accusation. Denial.
Condolences. Law. Corruption. Infidels. Forgery. Campaigns. Violence. A court ruling.
Al-Qaeda. Danger. Struggle. Hegemony. Refuge. Invasion. Route.)

The road is a gossamer thread:
    there is a sighted world swallowed by a blind one.
The cities are a death rattle, and time is a hoopoe passing by.
How long will you go on sleeping, sky cradled in red earth?

(Missiles. Gangs. Sects. Rituals. Attacks. Land mines. Commerce. Sectarian fighting.
Shelling. Cession. De-escalation. Sovereignty. Profiteering. Severed limbs. Corpses.
Battles. Allies. Enemies. Armed men. Assassinations. Tribes.)

Invisible hands snatch a child shaped like a coffin and carry him in the direction
    of no direction.
                Tell the eternal one,
"Your troupe performing this drama
is made of a mud called murder;
they wear a fabric called air."

(Oil. Uranium. Sound barrier. Ammunition. Scandals. Interrogation. Smuggling.
Laws. Right. Left. Negotiations. Betrayal. Torture. Evacuation . . . Etc.)

"The moon has an erotic wound, a gash made by politics," said an astronomer.
"The earth has punctures that imitate human orifices," said a biologist.
Between the two conjectures, Mount Judi became a red veil wrapping Noah's Ark.[10]
The air stomped its heels and synchronized its dance with the flow of atomic dust.
Threads and wires weave electronic capes

for strangers unfamiliar with the land
and whom the land does not recognize.
Piles of books stand tall. Under them lie the skulls of arguments inscribed by the pen
of miracle.
I did not tell the angels about this. I told a silent meteor that flickered briefly then
went out again.

Some were tainted;
                        their outsides became their insides.
Some read a great deal
                        and were soon inflicted with ignorance of all things.
And there was a third whose fourth
                        was none other than his shadow.

Horror played itself on the sun's lute.

"O Prophet of God, who will be first to enter paradise?
—The prophets.
—And then who?
—The martyrs.
—And then who?
—The muezzins of Bait al-Maqdis."[11]

"No one can be considered a martyr
on land or sea, unless he hears the call of
the muezzins of al-Quds in the heavens."[12]

"The rock of al-Quds lies atop a date palm
and the palm floats on a river from paradise,

and in the palm's shade sits Asiya, the pharaoh's wife,[13]
and Mary, daughter of Imran,[14]
until the Day of Judgment,
making beaded necklaces for those bound for paradise."[15]

What do we write then, and how?
Is there meaning for what will not enter language?
And why are the mind's sorrows mere graves for the body's desires?

—We will not succeed at writing anything
            unless we see it
            staring back at us.

—Writing that has no chasms, has no identity.

2. A SKY ON EARTH

Al-Quds, a dream-language.

A language that history bleeds into what came before it and after it, that mixes the human and the real, ending and non-ending. It is soil and water—you may knead as much as you wish.

(. . .)

"... God spoke to Moses on the ground of al-Quds.

God pardoned David and Solomon on the ground of al-Quds.

God gave Solomon back his kingdom in al-Quds.

God prophesied to Zacharias the birth of John the Baptist in al-Quds.

God gave David command over mountains and birds in al-Quds.

Gog and Magog will conquer the whole earth, except al-Quds,

and God will annihilate them on the ground of al-Quds.

Mary, peace unto her, received the fruit of winter in summer and the fruit

of summer in winter in al-Quds.

Jesus, son of Mary, peace unto him, was born and spoke in the cradle in al-Quds;[1]

the Last Supper descended to him in al-Quds;

and God raised him to the heavens from al-Quds,

and he shall descend from the heavens to al-Quds.

Abraham, peace be upon him, migrated from Kutha to al-Quds.[2]

God transported the Prophet Muhammad to al-Quds.[3]

Migration at the end of time will lead to al-Quds.

The Sirat bridge between hell and heaven begins in al-Quds.[4]

Israfil the archangel will blow his bugle in al-Quds,[5]

and the whale on whose back spreads the earth—
> its head where the sun rises, its tail where it sets—
> its midsection lies below the ground of al-Quds.[6]

The earth will fall into ruin, and rising remains al-Quds.
The first spot inhabited on earth was the rock of al-Quds.

Moses's spring will gush again at the end of time in al-Quds . . ."[7]

❀

. . . It is the ability to turn a whale into a canary, and a cow into a scythe for harvesting.

". . . And by that way wend the herds innumerable of bellwethers and flushed
ewes and shearling rams and lambs and stubble geese and medium steers and roaring
mares and polled calves and longwoods and storesheep and Cuffe's prime springers
and culls and sowpigs and baconhogs and the various different varieties of highly
distinguished swine and Angus heifers and polly bullocks of immaculate pedigree
together with prime premiated milchcows and beeves . . ."[8]

(. . .)

". . . and there is ever heard a trampling, cackling, roaring, lowing, bleating,
bellowing, rumbling, grunting, champing, chewing, of sheep and pigs and heavyhooved
kine . . ."[9]

(. . .)

"And all came with nimbi and aureoles and gloriae, bearing palms and harps and
swords and olive crowns, in robes whereon were woven the blessed symbols of their
efficacies, inkhorns, arrows, loaves, cruses, fetters, axes, trees, bridges, babes in a bathtub,
shells, wallets, shears, keys, dragons, lilies, buckshot, beards, hogs, lamps, bellows,
beehives, soupladles, stars, snakes, anvils, boxes of vaseline, bells, crutches, forceps,

stags' horns, watertight boots, hawks, millstones, eyes on a dish, wax candles, aspergills,
unicorns . . . chanting the introit in *Epiphania Domini* which beginneth *Surge,*
illuminare [O Jerusalem] . . .
> which saith
> de Saba venient.[10]

What is this head pulverized by raving, this body ripped by the claws of delusion? Is
man merely a myth of blood and flesh?
> Skeletons, skulls, veins, arteries, ears, eyes:
> tools and machines the dust preserved under its clothes and pillow.
> Each tool has teeth of gold, like verses that sculpt the gold of speech.

If dust knew how to stand on its feet, the sky
> would have been a mere thin anklet circling its heel.

Why is astonishment fading now? Why is time surrendering to its afflictions? If
eternity exists it must be the ancient ice, a brother to dust. And look, on every doorstep
and in every crossroad someone dead is confounding his coffin:
> Will the angels raise him
> or must he carry them instead?

❁

. . . Al-Quds, al-Quds,
> in your Bronze Age the apple was a woman.
> In your petroleum-electronic age the apple has become a bomb:
> > a transformation
> > where missiles only target lovers' homes.

And the lovers? Some pack their papers and head to the Stone Age, some pack their
papers and are lost
    not knowing whether to go and to where,
    or how to find direction.

The angels of certainty flee the bosoms of the planets and come to you, al-Quds.
They wash in your waters, and bow to your date palms. They grab the sky by the hair and
bring her to you. Sky torn away from sky, and their ropes choke the earth's throat.

A demographic balance!

People come to al-Quds from the ends of the world.
They plant themselves in its mud and water.

Three newcomers for every resident native.
The native departs, and the newcomer establishes
a demographic balance!
There is no Babel here, or Ashur.[11]
It's demolition, of stone and people.
It's politics—a new architecture.
No east in East al-Quds;[12] the villages around it are mist.
Secluded pockets encircled by every kind of police.
And where is international law?
It does not allow this; it considers it a crime.
But why does it remain silent?
Perhaps it's cooperating with this "silent expulsion."[13] Or merely echoing it?

❁

Al-Quds, fractures, buckles—
The Holy Basin, the Historical Basin,[14]
The city's reliquaries,
the foot of Mount Olive,
Silwan,[15]
Wadi Hilwa,[16]
The Bustan neighborhood,[17]
Sheikh Maddah neighborhood,[18]
Wadi al-Rababa, . . . etc., etc.[19]
Newcomer, plant yourself here!
Uproot yourself, O Native Son:
This is the refrain in God's music:
Glory to Solomon's stables![20]
Wander about, O Steeds of the angels, and nicker to your hearts' desire.

❋

The belly of the place bloats,
and Time devours embryos and their wombs.
What are these shadows the sun knows nothing of?
What are these bells that deny their own tolling?
And what is this theological Narcissus mirrored on the clouds?
Indeed, between language and reality there are trenches that cannot be filled.

Welcome to Nothingness, our king!

Mary, there is no life in life,
no life except in images.

Tomorrow who will greet you with peace
in these darknesses that embrace and bond?
The lung of speech leaves its ribcage
and between two walls—weeping and wailing—
the train of history comes and goes.

And Stars, why, why do you go on with your lying?

❧

Roads like trenches on the face of meaning,
gouged by the emperors' chariots.
Around them people celebrate,
around them platforms laden with machinery and banners,
around them coffins and diggers and graves.
The gods' blood hemorrhages,
the blood of childhood coagulates.
Teach us, dear Earth, how to wash off this stain.
Will we forever be stunned and dragged
behind the legions of our ancestors?

❧

"There is something on this earth worth living for,"
        says Zarathustra in Nietzsche's tongue.
Where is it then,
the gavel of liberty?
Where is the anvil of mind?

How can man, creator of meaning,
draw his destiny into one utterance?
                              How can his spirit
be poured into a wall?

❀

No one knows anything of it except the name,
as if objects existed only as utterances.
Skin devours pulp;
dust is another name for the Unknown.

And worst of all is man's wretchedness:
He descends into the vessel of "You, You,"
and rises as mist of "I am
at your beck and call,
your beck and call!"[21]

And here you are, *Jerusalem*–al-Quds
skating on the ice of meaning.
The sky houses her jinn and ifrits in you,
and they reign over the oceans of language.

❀

From a grave, from an etching, from a blade of grass shaped like a pair of breasts, from algae climbing a moist wall

a scent rises where gentleness and slavery mingle, and around them demons and
angels dance like a roiling surf.

Denied my daily loaf, I love being a hurricane and an earthquake inside you,
and I witness your end and your endlessness in one pulse,
and I declare nature's imprint on you:
> habit, sex, and intuition.

3. A ROPE BETWEEN A CAMEL AND A TANK

A. History/The Narrator

"Al-Waqidi (d. 207 H), al-Yaquobi, al-Tabari, Ibn al-Batriq, al-Istukhri, al-Massoudi, al-Maqdisi, Ibn 'Assakir, Osama ibn Munqid, al-Imad al-Isbahani, Yaqout al-Hamawi, Ibn al-Athir, Abu Sha'ma, Ibn al-'Ibri, Ibn Fadhl al-'Umri, Ibn Khaldoun, al-Maqrizi, Ibn Shahin, Ibn Taghribirdi, Shamsuddin al-Suyuti, Majr al-Din al-Ḥanbali al-'Ulaymi (d. 928 H).[1]

"These men, all of them, drew an image of al-Quds, delighted in its presence inside them and proselytized its meaning."

B. Summary/The Analyst

"They said, Al-Quds in a Muslim imagination is not earth. It is a sky, a paradise.

"A Muslim dissolves in her image: he exists not in himself but in that image. In her he abandons himself, roves displaced in her language—which is all of language. His words about her do not issue from him, but from that image through his tongue. It is that image-imagination speaking when he speaks."

C. Documentation/The Debt

"Whoever wants to see a spot of heaven, let him gaze at al-Quds."[2]

Earth—

Inside every stone a tank procreates, in each tree a bomb encamps. Above them hangs an oracle in the shape of red smoke.

From the Mediterranean, this one inimitable sea, the jaundice of our time gushes and glows.

Walls overfill with the hemispheres and empty their own secrets. A universe of straw and sulfur. Idols ally and conspire against human speech. Puppets slaughter each other below them. Here and there a stage to impale human beings on angel horns.

Slow down, deluge where paradise spins alone in orbit.

Look up, dear spheres, look at the shores or to the heights. Can you see a man or a woman? The moment is cutthroat iron, every medicine is a disease unto itself.

Three times, the earth shuddered in the mouth of the sky and millions of times the mouths of human beings trembled. Among the unknowns of the universe there is no egg protruding from the slit of a prophetic female, ready to fall in the lap of a divine cock.

Still, I suspect that one evening soon I will meet her barefoot, this female of the unknown in the garden of poetry. Together we will say to the hand of love, "Comb the hair of al-Quds, give her the mirror of poetry to see herself reflected in it."

Al-Quds, how strange that you give birth only
to yourself, even as the world's vulva sways
between your thighs.
                    Your bosom is shaped
like a grave, your throat like an explosive shell.
What song will unite your seasons
into a single pulse?   Where is the road that will recite your steps
like a holy book?
I ask you,
                    and I know that the question is woe itself.

What if we counted the skulls that tumbled and rolled (in your name) into history's tunnels and coliseums? Will they not be enough to raise another sky the size of our sky?

Shall we say then, "Blessed be the heavens whose thirst cannot be slaked except with earthly blood"? And shall we say, "Blessed be this earth that can only praise the heavens by being another graveyard"?

Beware, Passersby: for each of you alive on earth an abyss awaits you in that sky.

Ah, al-Quds, if you could see how human lungs are ripped, young and old, men's and women's, scattered among tourists' shoes and heaps of prayer, how the day of doom is extemporized in your name, how the wombs of all things turn into corpses and severed limbs, how houses and streets and the very air itself quake as continuous divine shelling fulfills divine prophecies and commandments, how unarmed creatures, insects and reptiles, flee the horror to the shadow of hope or the ambush of prayer!

"Do not kill the bat! For it sought the sea's permission to extinguish the fires when Bait al-Maqdis burned."[3]

(And these words may have been completed as:

"And do not kill the toad, for his croaking is prayer and hymn.")[4]

If only you'd see, al-Quds, how trees and flowers are gashed and torn, how fields are swallowed whole, willows shelled, how stones scamper to the embrace of their mother earth, far, far away from you, al-Quds.

The horizon now moans, quaking in fear, anticipating the aftershocks. Each end is a beginning, but you teach your sons nothing except death. What sort of life is it to be a hostage in a divine cage?

No, I am not afraid;

I fear nothing except your throngs whose lips cling to death's teats.

It's as if you are a horse whose limbs and organs are fighting each other in one battlefield, for one victory, for the One, their hooves dance on the corpses of other parts.

Oh, this endless feast! The dynasty of a single sky, its head devours its feet, its canines tear what remains.

This is how you till the emptiness. You'll not produce a miracle or a sign. There's nothing in your body but these fissures, and your blood is in the throes of a slow, slow death.

Have the skies wronged you? Or do you know a greater sinner, more arrogant and more lethal than yourself, al-Quds?

Here are your regions: they can be measured only with severed limbs.

"Silence, Poet! Silence!"

A pirate holds the moon by the hand and prepares for conquest. Will the sky not gasp in anger,

and scream,

"No. There is no hope in me, and I am no sky."

4. A BRIDGE TO JOB

A. Alley of the Moroccans

Can that museum, "the Museum of the Wailing Wall," ever welcome a swallow, or shake the hand of the Mediterranean, as Cadmus and Ulysses did? Will it ever know how to bring a woman back to life, the woman Europe was named after?[1]

Peace unto you, Human Steps, you have become an architecture that stands for nature.

Indeed, history has lower levels and rungs. Dust mocks the truths of water.
But what sort of history is this that cannot distinguish tears from ink, or a nail from a letter of the alphabet?

An engraving on a skull, not on clay. Echoes of mumbled divinations never recorded. Spume that topples the throne of water.

O for this system that can only rise when leaning on its stumps! And on Solomon's swamps sails a ship, not from the West or the East.[2]

From the dust of meaning.

Baptize yourself in these swamps then.

No harbor, no refuge in the Alley of the Moroccans except language — an open wound, like the book of Job.

Tell me, Book of Job:

Imprisonment. Assault. Torture. Starvation. Expulsion. Exile. Murder —

are these the spoons you left on your elegant and sumptuous tables?[3]

B. Song

A man who loves his shackles,
a wife fully veiled,
a girl wearing a headscarf,
and halal meat.
A hotel, a restaurant, a coffee shop, a graveyard.
No contradictions except
between an apple and Averroës.[4]
Table where the earth's bosom trembles below, writhe in hunger for a spoonful
scooped from the belly of the whale, or seek a path to that angelic swamp. You soothe
history with colors. You paint an image for the staff that became a serpent, for the sea to
open its thighs and let drifters pass, for the mountain that hosted Noah, his Flood and his
Ark, for the terror that no canvas can portray and that mocks all our colors.

Writhe in hunger, O Table where the earth's bosom trembles below, wail out your
hunger pangs.

C. Reflections

What can the children say to this ball they kick around and call life? How do they
grasp the world while the chains that grip their necks are mined from the pits of the
Unknown?

Traces of divination undulate in the book of Job: gardens, rivers of honey, effeminate
boys, and the remains of books erased by other writing.

To the battlefield, Angel Soldiers!

The commanders are swimming in the dust in their underpants.

The curtain is black. No light to hold the windows in place.

D. Narrative

I have never seen the moon arrested and dragged to the harbor of holy books as I saw it on that day. It was like a pebble rubbed between fingers, not a precious stone that adorns fingers, but one that crowns our feet. Tired, it sat in its work clothes like an infant whose mother, the sun, denied her breast. It was held captive by the book of Job. The before and the after, cartilage and bone, in pavilions where birds of paradise take off and alight.

Apple skin
on which Eve's feet slip.
The mob cries out to the bow maker:
"Where is your bow?"[5]
The staff that became a serpent did not know that every alleyway in al-Quds is a storehouse filled with prayers, all contradicting each other, or that the prayers that hobble to climb their own ladder are impregnated with human moans and were released ages before the Flood.

E. Song

Who can read religion or write poetry,
            when the Unknown shatters the spine of the land,
"and the earth erupts her final quaking?"[6]
The earth, planet of our wayward days—
            angels in it, devils
and divinity, symbolized and felt—
            is it not our only womb?

F. News

A schoolboy crosses a checkpoint.
He defiles what ought never be defiled.
Prison will suffice him until he reaches old age.

In the alley the smell of blood seeps from ages before the Flood.
Civil servants inspect the spout,
monitored by soldiers.
Thirst here surrenders its knowledge only to helmeted heads.
On a mountain of garbage the atoms dance.

A crimson angel leads an electronic army
and every machine spreads a new plague.

G. A Saying

What wall are you pointing to, Book of Job?

This wall rises from sand that was never a labyrinth. It was once a sail, and in it the gold of law blended with the silver of architecture.[7]

It has fallen from towers that abut planets obscuring any possibility of a horizon. And now it stands as a rubble of barbed wire, a recklessness filling the air's skull.

The wall lives multiple lives in this ephemerality, this earth. In the hereafter it will be merely a military shirt, guarding a camp filled with captives being tortured by divine executioners.

Anxiety fills a northern crack in the wall, shaded by words that know the unknown and sleep that resembles waking. The sun above dares to confess her age and infirmity. And in the shadow of the wall, the sun looks out from a window facing the Mediterranean—a sea that has no middle ground,[8] only tomb or sky.

But how close the tomb appears!
> And how distant the sky!
What can I say?
No, there is no sky anymore.
> No *Sama'*.[9]
The *Seen* is a sword, the *Mim* mortality,
the *Alifs* are an oppressive ancestry.
The glottal stop a vast emptiness.

H. Questions

I ask you, Book of Job,
how can a person build a bridge between two sides
> when he sees only one of them?

What does a woman covered by a veil of cotton or silk say
> to a woman covered by a veil of steel?
(. . .)
"As for your male and female slaves whom you may have—you may acquire male and
female slaves from the pagan nations that are around you. Then, too, *it is* out of the sons
of the sojourners who live as aliens among you that you may gain acquisition, and out of
their families who are with you, whom they will have produced in your land; they also
may become your possession. You may even bequeath them to your sons after you, to
receive as a possession; you can use them as permanent slaves . . ."[10]
And I ask you finally:
What becomes of a nation administered by killing or established on crime?
(. . .)

"Woe to him that builds a town
with bloodshed,
and establishes it on injustice!"[11]

I. Other Questions

When I read you, Book of Job, I see
how it swings inside you, how it breaks,
this thin reed called humanity.

Is the other not the pulse of the infinite in you?
Is he not your other self?
Where do you end, and where is your other, O Book of Job?
Why do you not stop erasing it, as if you too never cease to erase yourself?

Are you a journey to the world's extremities?
If so, then you and the other are one.

But where is your other, and where do you end, O Book of Job?

5. DISSECTION

1. Solomon's Stables/The Marwanite Mosque

The ants too pray to Solomon. Every bird carries a message to one of his wives.[1] And Marwan,[2] he was among the first who trusted and had faith.

2. The Hill at the Moroccan Gate, Again and Again

Above it a cemetery hangs in the air suspended from a rope that ties the navel of the East to the lips of the West. A cemetery that almost hovers, filling the air with its moans. And between Buraq Square and the Haram al-Sharif, trees coated with dust release their laughter.[3]

The air is garrulous. It sleeps only in silent rooms, protected by guards in armored cars flung by the angels into the embrace of al-Quds.

3. The Wailing Wall/The Buraq Wall

The wailing is sometimes lightning, other times a buraq.

The two walls are perfumed by God's steps and his prophets' and messengers' (among whom we make no distinction).[4]

The red roses between the two walls veil themselves in black shade.

4. The Western Wall Tunnel/Tunnel at 'Ain Silwan/Tunnel at Wadi Hilwa

Torches held in the horizon's grasp illuminate the tunnels.[5]
Tunnels that disgorge death and swallow life.

Voices rise from the earth's gullet. A dialogue between Solomon, his hoopoe and Sheba's Bilqis.

The envious ants try to eavesdrop.[6]

5. The Synagogue of Ohel Yitchak

Ask prayer itself, and prayer will tell you:
"I would rather be a dance."

The ground where the synagogue stands complains.[7] The sounds of weeping rising from Hammam al-'Ain accompany it.[8] The al-Aqsa Mosque joins the wailing. The Tankiz Khan can never find water for his ablutions, always misses the late night prayer.[9]

He slips away to Buraq Square and watches out for the angels of sadness to arrive . . .

6. Beit Hetslam/Beit Sharon

What is the use of a house that has no water, not even air?[10] Not even a bird flying around it.

Shshshsh! There's a soldier pretending to be a column over there.

7. Bab al-'Amud/Damascus Gate

What if the dictionary swung to and fro and fell apart, and the gate became a column/'*amud*, and the column, a gate?

The Roman road places its cap on the Damascus Gate, holding a flower and heading toward the al-Wad Street promenade—the Cardo, Documenas Maximus, Byzantium, the Ummayad Caliphate, the Abbasid Caliphate, the Crusaders, the Ayyubites, the

Mamluks, the British—you can hear their voices today, and even now see the rooms where they slept and the beds of their concubines.[11]

8. Solomon's Cave/Magharat al-Kittan

Is a woman's dress part of her skin?
I admit to a sip of alcohol in my question.
Can Solomon speak to his cave?[12]

9. The Land of Sabra

How strange the earth's anguish.[13]
It does not tear apart the earth, but tears apart those walking above it.

10. The Souk al-Khawajat

What are they doing, these memories rummaging through garbage? A pair of pants here, a gazelle's horns there.[14]

11. Burj al-Laqlaq/Stork Tower

Music weeps between storks' wings.[15] A dance apologizes to their nests.

12. 'Ain Silwan/Silwan Spring

Magic in Palestine has an eye-spring that no eye can see.[16]

13. Land of Siyyam

There is no harm in delaying your fast, dear horizon.[17]
Break it, and bring down the rain.

14. Wadi al-Nar/Wadi Hilwa

The fire of the valley is a valley of fire. Each valley is a pool, but Wadi Hilwa is a question.[18]

15. Talat al-Dhuhour (David's City)

Strange, how the city of David agreed to have its name switched to Talat al-Dhuhour![19] How was the continent of language not struck with an earthquake?

Dear Tanks, dear Bombs, a force commands you, "Tear the people up first then the other creatures, but kindly. Name your attack a defensive act or an attempt to seek peace. You know that here God is a fabulous being and the devil is a realistic one. Scream, then! And Believer, you must escape reality. Why do you live it in the first place?

Escape, escape to what lies behind."

16. 'Ain Um-al-Darj Spring

A woman who is not a fish or a genie or a nymph lives contented in this spring.[20]

17. Chain Street

A chain of dove wings gently drags a wounded comrade.[21]

18. Al-Wad Street

Who knows how to hide inside his own voice?

19. Via Dolorosa

Nothing was ever created. Everything created in Palestine begins at this road.[22] And graves are the semen of al-Quds.

20. Qubat al-Sakhra/Dome of the Rock

Can Palestine release a more powerful cry than the dome of the world crowning its head? Will it suffice Palestine that its tears pierce the rock of Creation?

Her daylight rides the mare of night
and her night is ridden by the Buraq:
    Some travel is history
    and some mere conjecture.
With each transgression an abyss of depravity gapes.
What to make of this world/uterus, child, grave/grave, uterus, child?
Take her in a swirl,
               inside a triangle,
                   however you wish, whenever you wish,
    no end
    but this endlessness.

A dove soars under the dome and the dome's solitary lamp flutters like a moth winged with flame.
A man and a woman embrace,   white   black . . .   Wait for the colors of birth.
History, keep your hands down!   Eternity, raise yours up.

21. The Tunnel ('Ain Silwan/Wadi Hilwa, the Western Wall Tunnel— Again and Again)

A tunnel is to be born wherever you wish, even before you are born. You will have roots and kin you know nothing of, or their whereabouts. You will say, "What is above the tunnel is mine, and what is around it, before it, and after it, all mine!"

"Let the sky explode in rage," says the master of the tunnel.

And you can tell him, "I will choose the wind that will carry the magic carpet of meaning. And I will command the atmosphere to waft a soft breeze, pliable and obedient. As soon as it blows through a tunnel it goes through another, longer and deeper."

As to you, native son, ball yourself up inside your house. Do not leave until a guard's light shines from the tunnels and says, "Get out! There is no escape from this tunnel except to another, and the future is made of tunnels."

Children in this future are boxes, dummies, explosive canisters, cockroaches made of dynamite, iron

cooked with every kind of spice . . .

A swarm of names shoots out of the tunnel. This is what is written on their shirts: "From dust the Arabs came, and to dust they shall return."

The tunnel is a putrid history.

Even if you leave the tunnel to its emptiness, to trade again in what will be nothing but emptiness, the tunnel will not leave you.

"There are suns that rise only at night," the tunnel will say to you, handing you the rope of temptation.

Steal a glance at the beginning of the tunnel, and in it you will see your end.

The tunnel is another coffin.

The road leading to here is narrow, but it is not far from paradise.

History—an artificial water where ancestries and lineages spawn.

The tunnel speaks on everything, but never says a thing.

A blind man in the shape of an angel leans on the tunnel's gate:

"Is it true what they're saying here?"

"Oh, how is it that you dared to speak at last?"

"Go on, blind one!"

"The tunnel is filled with women, but there is only one womb among them.

The womb of a woman named Eve. Her husband divorced her, his name was Adam.
And the tunnel has only one lover: the wall,
    even though the tunnel has many tunnels within it."

"We are still swinging above the edge of the abyss,"
                                the blind one says again.
I cannot not tell him what I thought—
"Al-Quds was a shirt, until the Arabs all leapt to wear it,"
                                says the tunnel in my stead.

6. AFFLICTIONS

A. Questions

• Why is every atom of Palestine's ash an open wound? How does this wound create life with the implements of death?
• Is Palestine's history an autumn that has migrated beyond the seasons?
• Why does the face of humanity wrinkle in the language of Arab leaders? And why is this language clogged with trains that run only on dead-end tracks that never end? And why are those tracks built by leaders who wage battles on trees and water?

B. Letter to Ezekiel

Ezekiel, visionary and seer,
    look again and again.
    Ruin is still the daily bread of God's earth. Will the prophecies also turn into a siege? Will tunnels be burrowed into their words? Will their visions splinter into missiles and bombs, into volcanoes of gas and phosphor? Is it true, dear Ezekiel, that you have befriended this dragon?
    And I almost ask you, Have you met Salome? Why is the beast of the ages masquerading as the angel of eternity? And that poor donkey foal in Matthew's prophecy, why is it limping and falling?[1]
    And we, the concubine's children,[2] what must we do when the earth itself is a concubine in the grip of divine prophecies?
    Iron gushes, rising and falling on the ladders of prayer.
    Tumors and blubber are life's Adam and her Eve. The day's eyelashes burn and the minutes stone their origins.

Shall we save women's bellies and stow away their embryos?
Shall we say to their breasts, "Find another universe"?
Will chains emerge in between our steps?
Are wombs graves from now on?

Ezekiel, dear seer,
nothing matches your prophecies except thunder.
Please allow me to shout out,
"Salome,
blood is spilling on thresholds, walls, and windows.
You know the hearts of these masters, these prophets and politicians. Tell me,
what do their hearts actually pump?
                    How do they soften and when, and what is their secret?"
A rose longs for no perfume but its own.
A bird never flies carrying its nest.
The earth is mercy—and dust is the first and the last.
Why do the books deceive?
                    Why is every letter of the alphabet chained,
                                        every human mouth bridled?
Why can the sky not be seen except as
                                        owned, branded, tattooed, guarded, and walled?
Is it a stockyard for language?
Is it a storage room for the gold of prophecies?
Salome—Herodia—Hero-shima![3]
As soon as your name is pronounced, all senses are extinguished.
No, you are not the dance, not the lover, not a woman at all.

Forgive me, Ezekiel, dear seer.

C. Considerations

—How can you face the rock of al-Quds stained with urine and excrement?

—Go, cleanse your feet with light and repent.

"Fresh water and the pollen winds
issue from a rock below Bait al-Maqdis."[4]
Prophecies slake the thirst of chaos,
and toss their flowers in the streets,
where the poets are wolves and mercenaries, and where we Arabs raid cities singing
in unison:
> On one bed, we conquer a hotel,
> with one hotel, we make a continent.
> No matter that our feet rise
> higher than our prayers
> even the sun envies us.
> Praise be to God who favored us!

How wretched the likes of me—
> and I am no Job,
> I am no golden mouth.

D. Omega (Palestinian-Jewish)

How lovely![5] Palestine's stars stroll in Jerusalemite denim! How lovely that an Arab
planet skates on top of the Wailing Wall wearing a tattered veil!

How lovely that African cocoa sates Palestine's desires!

Meanwhile atomic clouds glide above, and the veil is the fatwa of the hour.

Where do they come from, these swift fists pummeling the face of the Unknown?

Are they angels' heads? From a nuclear hell? From the Day of Judgment? From the Holy Basin?

The Holy Basin—Holy Uterus[6]—the star of the past ovulated and the future burrowed into her.

The clouds whispered in the poet's ear:

> "Do not believe this.
> How could God need rest?
> A god of the throne?
> Is there a throne that would fit him?
> Will he need mattresses and cushions?
> Does he have a colt to ride?
> Does he take the land of one son
> and give it to the other?"

"Nothing leads to wisdom except the parable of the tree," nature tells the poet. "Not Adam's tree. But a tree neither in heaven nor hell, 'neither from the East, nor from the West.'"

"But beware," nature goes on, "of that winged creature behind you. His lips are a pair of lambs, but he flings a knife or a hatchet with every word. You are right, dear Poet, to doubt that they are human, those creatures that don Adamic heads on their shoulders."

"I will throw a rope for you to climb, or to dance on, from the ends of the earth to the beginning of the sky, from the ends of the sky to the beginnings of the earth," said the wilderness to the poet.

"And you will distill your fragrance, your poetry, from a plant that grows around women's waistlines." Only lying will be truthfulness then. You will exclaim, and invariably others will echo your words:

What a slaughter the sky is!
What rot the earth has become!

E. A Hymn Bracing for the End

Many gray hairs on my head,
but in my insides only the down of childhood.
Take away your alchemy, dear Poetry, raise it, discipline it, and teach it to mingle our
bodies with our dreams,
how time can earn a place among our days and nights,
how minutes grunt in our veins like wild horses.
In your name, I flee myself to be myself,
and in your name I become joy and sadness in one inhale,
and I clamp my lips on your secrets.

The sky hangs like a rare painting in the earth's museum
and each is fighting to prove he alone stole it.
Up high, the sky's seventh ceiling bucks and shudders, about to fall.
Why are harlots and pimps given another great role to play?
And in the name of the sky, must we awaken Job, Jeremiah, and Isaiah to display their
afflictions again in al-Quds, and to confess how happy and free they once were?

Go on your way, dear Heaven.
Leave me a while to check on my limbs.

7. TEMPTED BY NOTHING: A SONG

I do not believe the mind of the crowd
I believe in light—
              radiating, penetrating, pointing a direction.

Dear Tree of Knowledge,
how can I brother the forests of al-Quds to me?
And who is this One who is never present
          except at funerals or on a throne?

Not yet.
The disaster has not arrived.
                  The flood has yet to burst.
The Mediterranean is readying itself. The oceans stamp and shudder.
Who will gift this marble head to the king of trades?[1]
Who will say to Hannibal:
          "Rome defeated you, but you are the victor.
          And from your skull another dawn rises now."

My body is not ether.
My body is dust and bone.
A physics of arteries and veins.
I live in a hut of smoke, and I wear clouds for clothes.
Endless and without ever succeeding, I try to heal the sky.

What a criminal I must be, living innocently like rain.
My only sin is that I compete with light.

Shut yourself up before me, dear Sky.
You will never see me at your door again.

And you, dear Planets, I will not ask you again to be
                              a ladder for my steps.
Inside me countless planets abide.

And now, Lover, strike up your song!

❀

Is your throat your lover? Is your lover your throat?

Don't answer. Just sing.

Time tumbles, stone by stone from the hand of its god.
His children are mountains of weeping.

I see a star above your head, dimming.
I sense sails being ripped in the lakes of your dreams.

Sing!

❀

Waves take shape in your features. You sing the tide's ebb and flow.
Praise be to song!
Praise be to love!
Right and wrong are a pair of twins between them,
and the truth
is their shared wound.

     Here he is ringing the bell of meaning,
      but will anyone listen?
What good will it do, the hand you reach out to us, O Sun?

Sing, Lover!
Prophecies scamper away from you, jealous near insane.
To you alone belongs life's ageless allure.

It's true, the firmament in al-Quds resembles a cage: the whole universe in a mere one thousand square meters.[1]

Piles of papers stand at each crossroad, shaped like books. Ink spills out of them at the speed of twenty centuries for each letter, thirty centuries a comma, and countless centuries a period.

Oh what a pile Solomon's hoopoe is pecking through! Line by line.

Have the holy books fallen into the abyss?

"The rock of al-Quds is a stone from paradise."[2]

(Greek Orthodox. Copts. Assyrians. Chaldeans. Roman Catholics. Armenians. Abyssinians. Kurds. Turks. Circassians. Moroccans. Refugees. Farmers. Civilians. City folk. Jews. Arabs . . .)

(Humidity. Heat. Falafel. Frankincense. Settler colonization. Occupation. Doves. Pigeons. Cars. Pepsi-Cola. Minarets. Bells . . .)

One square kilometer, no more!

"The gate of al-Quds is the land of summoning and resurrection."[3]

"Whoever prepares for the pilgrimage
from the al-Aqsa Mosque in Jerusalem
to the Masjid al-Haram in Mecca, God will forgive his past
and future sins, and paradise is guaranteed him."[4]

❀

The house bids its memory farewell,
                and the dust around it lifts its sleeves
in wind that ruffles the days' heads
with violence, with locusts that devour the shoots of time.

Women had planted their wombs into dream earth
and commissioned God with the task of reaping.
Some of them die at nightfall and are reborn at dawn,
some write a lover's sighs with the patience of the sages,
some wear yokes, mistaking them for fur collars.

❀

No sound except what issues from hurricanes banging
                against metal, and light bouncing
                in confusion from one metal to another.
Ghosts assemble and disassemble under the armpits of space.
The Mediterranean sits up on its atomic throne, or the very throne of God.
Veined hands wrestle over the blubber of time. The body of desire stands on a metal
platform. Its spirit lies sprawled on the asphalt.
And you, dear Water,
when will you separate yourself from clay?

Night, scatter your stars over al-Quds.
The prophets of insomnia sleep among her severed limbs. At her feet
mud stands, then breaks apart into deserts and ravines.

What will happen to those divine tablets that descended to al-Quds?
What will happen to the devils and their armies,

                      to the angels and their gods?

What will happen to the earth and her children?

Does anyone know al-Quds, except her stars?

PART II *Images*

First Image of the Meaning of al-Quds

How do we apologize to roses our feet trampled,
roses lying around the city's eyelashes?
Blocked roads   books oozing blood   and in the mud
                                        screams
                    the mouth of language could not explain.
How do we lay a blossom on its last pillow?   How do we infuse our love into
the arrogance of stone?
Gentle and wild this city's blood   blood that pours
into the cave of words no eye is wide enough to apprehend.

Space around us, lend your throat to a dove with broken wings!
Mask yourself with the crystals of our exhales,
                    and open your chest to us.[1]

All sorts of blood can read and write,
all kinds of ruin improvise their shapes and colors.
Many, many women swim the lakes of remembrance.
The oblivion of soldiers.   The wheezing of the barracks.

Eternal one, why are you sweeping
                all that is temporal
                        with the tip of your broom,

throwing it into an inferno of horror?
Why do you offer the angels only the devil's poison to drink?

He
does not know how to hold a rifle;
he draws his wounds on wings of light.

All things come to an end;
they descend the ladders of infinity.   The days are notebooks, their sheets
                                                                                            blow
in soundless distances.   How can he teach his face
to return to its childhood?
Embers burn in his innards   embers in his history   embers in
                                                                                            his steps.
And what is this alliance between heaven and money?

Second Image

Advance, Stranger,   enter the city from any corner   from any
direction.   Till, plant, and harvest   what you wish   when-
ever you wish   however you wish.
                        Welcome!   Take what is yours.[2]

Along the road there is only gold that uproots the mind,   or silver
          that erects prison towers in air, light, and water.
Law is a slave to everything except itself.   Lying is the master of the universe;
          honor has no code.
And oh how horrid your suffering, dear Sincerity!

At my lips is a loaf named reality,
in my hand a coin that writes our works and days.
Which colors will draw your portrait, dear Truth?

Third Image

Is the Arab sky on the street a new Helen?   Bare breasts
wild thighs,   all her lovers descendants of the gods.
No fear   no guardianship.   Attack and raid!
    A time that knows no worship
    other than the prayers of the dead.
Do you want to be described as a believer?
Then you must kill.

What is this cancerous ghost dressed up as reality
    between the waters of the Ocean and the Gulf?[3]
    And Passerby, what do you prefer:
    the magic of imagination, or the magic of language?
And what is this "present" that awakens the past,
        and rearranges its days and events?
How can the alphabet embrace this new wilderness?

Nature like a broken sand tablet
    scattered by the fingers of a blind storm.
No sound
    except the clanging of metal, and light
    like a seagull shivering in terror bouncing
from one metal to another. Small ghosts

crawl under the arms of space.
                    Wheels lurch forward,
powered by human bodies. In the distance, the fields spread
like cushions and mattresses for nuclear thrones,
                    kingdoms that expand by the will of God.

The horizon is dusty and disheveled,
an iron necklace dangles from its neck:

                    Only iron speaks the truth.

Fourth Image

Clay rises, erects itself into a mountain, then divides into tribes and clans.

Tablets and myths. Signs and tokens. A demon in each fruit, and the human face is the first fruit to fall.

Time is pulverized. Is there anywhere in this nowhere?

History arrived, invited by ash.
It roamed   saw   and inquired.
The roads blacken   the doors open up.   Words
are bombs and prayers.
No color in the bird wings that flash through the horizon's arcades.
No wings on the birds.
No birds.

—How do we combat the savagery of the interior with the savagery of the exterior?
—Accuser/Accused: How do I live between two blades racing to kill me?
—Are accusations and executions a national sport?
—Do you want to be honest today? Start lying then.

They   have become excellent at taxidermy.
They do not only embalm bodies   they embalm
minds and ideas   and now they intend
to embalm light   not only

exterior light   but also the light of inner life.
"No one can vanquish us"; this is how they describe themselves.

No locks on the houses they built   and left
as inheritance for their sons.   The houses were the locks themselves.
        And the ancestors who spread their shadows now
are rolled back like scrolls,[4]   their traces carried from generation
to generation   from house to house   in clothes   in dishes
even in spoons   but mostly in tongues and brains.
Men like pieces of luggage
of whom it is said, "They committed not a single sin among them,
                and left their children only an inheritance of good deeds,"
blessed be their feet and their steps,
        as they move like ships riding the clouds
        assured a profit of bliss.
What will the scales measure?   What stories will the candles tell?
        And what are they jabbering, these human sediments?
Men — it is said — who reside in perfection, in proportion, in fullness
resting on couches covered with lizard skin!

Dear Facts coming toward us,
you'll never have the luck to follow their path.
Nonetheless,
nature's army does not cease to raid their fortresses
supported always by the armies of habitude.

Cover them with your care, dear Emptiness!

Their water does not run:
It does not long for its sibling, the air.
And even their language laments,
    "In each of my words
    sits a tyrant
    and a human being with a slit throat.
    In each of my alphabets
    a hunted corpse
    and a dead nightingale.
    How did I, angelic all my life,
    acquire these demonic teeth?"

They say, "The world is preserved in words engraved on the trunk
                    of an apple tree
    and sung by the earth's flutes."

    "A flute, like the serpent, that can turn into a staff,"
        whispered a passerby who did not say his name.

I know the body, muscle by muscle, cell by cell.
Still I ask it:
    "Who gave you these lips?"

Many questions press against me. I present them to those people,
    especially to them,
  and I have many answers that do not obey me.
    I will remain a friend to all questions,
        and I will not compromise with the answers.

A history of others' steps—
such provisions do not suit me.
I need only what the body's history can give.

Come and discover my insides.

                                  Brother me to you, dear Doubt.

What can we do
when coincidences are our only proofs?

Fifth Image

Venus shines on the ankle of a woman named Venus.
A moon grins back at a dog barking at him.
Why is your waist trembling, dear City?
Now I understand why the sky sways like a curtain at times
        and like a sunflower too.
And you,
Great being of perfection, fullness, and judgment,   lead us—
        Where are you leading us?
And where is the music of our departure?
And who will side with us when it plays?
Murder—the master sport:

murder for an eye	for a tooth	for a nose	for a chest
murder for a hand	for a foot		
murder with a tongue	with a word	with a throne	with bread

with a drink of water.[5]

Murder for the slaves at your command.[6]

Murder to improve the race   to perfect the mind—
("They were killed   hacked!")
        Lift this head off the table   set it aside
                examine it.

Make sure
    it has no residue of thought or dream
      that could muddle the images the creator purportedly followed
        to make his creation.
  Virile murder
  so the sky may widen, and the cities of date palms bloom
  blossom   by blossom   by blossom.
  Sweat falls from the day's bosom.   A horde of wolves
  and rabbits climb the columns of history.   Smoke
from explosives, thick and wide.   Time is a panther growing old and frail.
  His ears fall, his teeth and his incisors fall.
His shoulders too—Can he stretch out a leg to shake hands with death?
Attack!   Raid!   Enter houses through their roofs.
  May the red heifer also enter the body of language with you![7]
         May her bull mate and his sons also enter.
      Let them storm the streets and alleyways.   Let them
all sleep on the bed of our imagination.
Let in herds of images
  and the shepherds of meaning too.

  Language, listen to me please!
         I want to break the anvil of paper
     with the hammer of ink.
And think, dear Poet, of the ductile metal and flame
blazing inside holy verses   the pummeling that does not cease
to dream or dance   of the dictionary being rewritten
by the languages of massacre and divination   of the city that heaven sent
as a princess to rule all other cities.

Think!   Let your thoughts germinate under a colorless veil.
Remember and remind:
The elephant of migration is butting its head against the road and the tribes'
                              spears[8]—
Rumble/Whir/Crack/Drone:
                    the racket of angels drilling holes
through the walls of earthly life.

No Babylon   but streets and houses that are cemeteries and caves.
No Babylon   but a sexual history for nonsexual organs.
No Babylon   but the backbone of a phoenix cracking under a nightmare of ash.
No Babylon   but days that are "ruins" guarded by green idols.
No Babylon   but endless flocks of *ababil.*

Oh My Soul who has gone and yet to return,
                        shall I say what others have said?
"Please reinvent me, dear mirage!"

Sixth Image

Ropes braided by the history of murder   droop from the city's balconies
and from them we hang.

Around us wingless birds gather and mockingly ask,
"Why?
And how is it that you do not fly?"
Delusion.   Delusion.
        We doubt that we have hands and feet—
(Are there hands and feet not shaped in the wombs of murder?)

You who are called human   the politics of legitimacy
        can rename you a mouse or whale   or turn you into a sack in which
        beliefs are poured like garbage.   You will never hear
        Adam calling you "my dear son!"

No   I will not fall to the gravity of murder.

        God's earth,
what will you say about me when I refuse?
What will you do to me then?

Yes, I will be taken by the shooting stars glittering in the grotto
of love.

Taken by love.

Seventh Image

Death breeds and rebreeds,   death piles up on itself.
A grave retreats   a grave advances.
A headstone reads nature and what lies behind it.   The sky's nerves
comb through the earth's body
and instinct   becomes a paradise   where lead
                          is crowned king.
Erupt, dear Silver!   Tell the children   to become barricades.
      Tell women   to dive into the dough of desire.
Death piles up on itself   death breeds and rebreeds.
Quiet, dear Compass, and get back to work!   The music of bullets
is perfecting the art of eulogy.   A star riding a horse passes under
a bridge   carrying a doll called politics   a politics
of prostitution under a sky   patting prayers on their shoulders.

Who will test these ruins that broke their covenant with God?

A mountain sprints like the wind.
A river rises to drink the clouds.
But what will spring do in this city
among children who die, strangled or burned?
What can spring do in a language that refuses to read anything

but autumn?
And Hell, in which sky do you reside
and from which heaven will you descend?

NOTES

Unless otherwise indicated, all quotations from the Qur'an are taken from the translation by Abdullah Yusuf Ali, available online at the Quranic Arabic Corpus, http://corpus.quran.com/translation.jsp?chapter=1&verse=1. Citations give the Arabic name of the sura followed, where necessary, by its English name and then the verse numbers. References to the "Old City" are to the oldest section of al-Quds/Jerusalem. Unless otherwise indicated, dates are given in the order A.D./A.H. All ellipsis and suspension points are in the original.

1. Heavenly Summary

1. *Al-Quds* and *Bait al-Maqdis* are the Arabic words for Jerusalem. *Al-Quds* means "purity" and also "blessing." *Bait al-Maqdis* means the "house of purity and blessing." More specifically "Bait al-Maqdis" refers to the area where the al-Aqsa Mosque and the Dome of the Rock are situated. Al-Quds was the first *qibla* (the direction a person faces in prayer) for Muslims before the Qur'an commanded Muhammad to have Muslims pray facing Mecca instead. All of al-Quds is considered holy ground in Islam; the entire city is a house of worship, just as Mecca is viewed as holy ground and a place of worship. Because they see al-Quds as sacred ground, Muslims are not allowed to wage war there. During the Arab-Muslim conquest of al-Quds, the Muslim general Abu Ubaida ibn al-Jarah besieged the city until it surrendered in peace. And in A.D. 1187, during the Crusades, Saladin also refused to fight inside the city, besieging it until it surrendered.

2. This is a saying by Ka'b al-Ahbar, quoted in Majr al-Din al-Hanbali al-'Ulaymi, *Al-Uns al-jalil bi-tarikh al-Quds wa-al-Khalil*, edited and authenticated by Mahmoud 'Awdah al-Ka'abinah, under the supervision of Mahmoud Ali Ata-Allah (Hebron and Amman: Maktabat Dandis, 1999), p. 349, which cites *Ithaf al-ikhsa bi-fad'il al-masjid al-aqsa*, by the fifteenth-century scholar Shams-uldin Muhammad ibn Ahmad al-Suyuti (A.H. 813–880), vol. 1/hadith 137. Throughout these notes I use the edition *Ithaf al-ikhsa bi-fad'il al-masjid al-aqsa*, edited by Ahmad Ramadan (Cairo: al-Hay'a al-misriyah al-'ama lil-kitab, 1982); citations are given by volume/hadith. Ka'b al-Ahbar (full name Abu Ishaq Ka'b ibn Mati' al-Humyari al-Ahbar) was a prominent rabbi from Yemen who was one of the earliest important Jewish converts to Islam. (It was claimed that he converted during the time of the Prophet Muhammad, but the date has not been confirmed.) He is counted among the Tabi'in (the second generation of disciples) and narrated many Isra'iliyat, narratives brought into the Islamic tradition from Jewish and Christian sources. He was an in-

fluential figure in the reigns of the caliphs Umar ibn al-Khattab and 'Uthman ibn 'Affan, 634–656/12–36.

3. The poet here alludes to Qur'an, al-Anfal: The Spoils of War, 8:30: "And [remember, O Prophet,] how those who were bent on denying the truth were scheming against thee, in order to restrain thee or to slay thee, or to drive thee away: thus have they [always] schemed: but God brought their scheming to nought for God is above all schemers" (The Message of the Qur'an, trans. Muhammad Asad [London: Book Foundation, 2012]). Asad's translation is typical of most translations of the Qur'an, in which the translator attempts to minimize the force of the Arabic word makr. It does not mean simply "plan" or "scheme"; it also means "deceive," which is the meaning I preferred in this case.

4. The poet here is making an ironic allusion to the Islamic ascription of wisdom and mindfulness to ants because of their ability to speak—hence their status as higher than all the planets. This is based on the story of Solomon and the ants. Solomon was marching with his army of humans, jinn, and birds when he came upon an ant advising its community to enter their dwellings lest they be crushed by the army. Amused, Solomon gave thanks to God and redirected his forces away from the ants (Qur'an, al-Naml: The Ant, 27:17–19). Solomon, considered a prophet by Muslims, was celebrated for his wisdom and knowledge of the unseen, as well as of the traditional sciences of cosmology. According to tradition, he knew the "language of beasts and birds." Other supernatural abilities bestowed upon him by God included control of the wind and rule over the jinn (Qur'an, Sawd, 38:30–39).

5. This quotation is a hadith (saying of the Prophet) found in Shihab al-Din abi Mahmoud ibn Tamim al-Maqdisi (d. 1363/765), Muthir al-gharam ila ziyarat al-quds wa al-sham, quoted in al-'Ulaymi, Al-Uns al-jalil, p. 353.

6. This quotation is a hadith found in al-Maqdisi, Muthir al-gharam, quoted in al-'Ulaymi, Al-Uns al-jalil, p. 357.

7. "Imru-ulqais" (Imru al-Qays ibn Hujr al-Kindi) was an Arab poet who lived in the sixth century A.D. He is said to have been the first to submit Arabic verse to fixed rules and laid down laws for the rhymes. A prince, a freethinker, and a tragic figure, he wrote one of the Mu'allaqat (Suspended Odes), the seven suspended odes (qassidas) that were considered the best poems of pre-Islamic Arabia.

8. 'Ukaz was a town in the Arabian peninsula that held the most famous and important annual fair, principally for buying and selling and the exchange of various commodities, in pre-Islamic times. It was situated to the southeast of Mecca and strategically located in the middle of the spice route of western Arabia. 'Ukaz was significant in other, nonmaterial aspects as well. It was a unifying force among the Arab tribes, a place where contests, literary and other, were held, and where

covenants and contracts were made. It flourished during the sixth century. An important poetry contest was held in the market (souk) of 'Ukaz.

9. Hijaz is the region in western Arabia where Mecca and Medina, the holiest cities in Islam, are located.

10. Mount Judi, according to early Christian and Islamic tradition, is the place where Noah's Ark came to rest at the end of the Flood (Qur'an, Hud, 11:44).

11. "O Prophet of God . . . Bait al-Maqdis" is a hadith found in al-Suyuti, *Ithaf al-ikhsa bi-fad'il al-masjid al-aqsa,* 1/147, quoted in al-'Ulaymi, *Al-Uns al-jalil,* p. 356.

12. The quotation is a hadith found in al-'Ulaymi, *Al-Uns al-jalil,* p. 356.

13. The Qur'an version of the rescue of baby Moses on the banks of the Nile differs from the biblical version. In the Qur'an, Asiya, the pharaoh's wife, rather than his daughter discovers Moses and decides to adopt him. Asiya is one of the most revered women in Islam; she was thought to have been a monotheist, who worshipped God in secret despite being the Egyptian king's wife.

14. Mary, daughter of Imran, is the Qur'anic name for Mary, the mother of 'Issa or Jesus Christ (Qur'an, Aali-Imran: The Family of Imran, 3:35–47).

15. A hadith found in al-Suyuti, *Ithaf al-ikhsa bi-fad'il al-masjid al-aqsa,* 1/130, quoted in al-'Ulaymi, *Al-Uns al-jalil,* p. 357.

2. A Sky on Earth

1. The Qur'an states that Jesus ('Issa) first spoke when he was in the cradle to defend his mother against accusations that she had been with a man who fathered her child; she claimed that no man had touched her (Qur'an, Maryam: Mary, 19:27–33).

2. The poet refers to Kutha as Abraham's native city, rather than Ur, which is the more common attribution. Kutha (today's Tel Ibrahim) was an ancient Sumerian city located in Iraq, east of the Euphrates River and north of Nippur, twenty-five miles northeast of Babil Governorate. Kutha is also the capital of the Sumerian underworld.

3. "The Glory to (Allah) Who did take His servant for a Journey by night from the Sacred Mosque to the farthest Mosque, whose precincts We did bless, — in order that We might show him some of Our Signs: for He is the One Who heareth and seeth (all things)" (Qur'an, Isra: Ascension, 17:1). Muhammad then ascended to the heavens in what is known as his Mi'raj. Both the trip to Jerusalem and the Mi'raj occurred in a split second and are considered great miracles.

4. Al-Sirat is a bridge erected above the fires of hell that separates the dead from Paradise. The bridge bristles with hooks and thorns, and is narrower than a hair and sharper than a sword. The righteous are able to cross it, although how quickly they do so depends on their piety; sinners who worshipped false deities fall into the burning pit when they attempt to crawl over the bridge.

5. Israfil is the archangel who will blow the trumpet from a holy rock in al-Quds to announce the Day of Resurrection. The trumpet is constantly poised at his lips, ready to be blown when God orders. In Judeo-Christian biblical literature, Raphael is the counterpart of Israfil.

6. In some interpretations of the first verse of the sura al-Qalam: The Pen (68:1), "Nun" refers to a great whale that rides on the currents of the seas, carrying the earth on its back. See the commentary on the Qur'an by Ibn Kathir ('Imad al-Din abi al-Fida Isma'il ibn Kathir), *Tafsir al-Qur'an al-azim*, available online in Arabic at http://quran.al-islam.com/Page.aspx?pageid=221&BookID=11&Page=1, and in English at https://archive.org/details/TafseerIbnKathirenglish114Surahs Complete.

7. The poet, quoting al-'Ulaymi, *Al-Uns al-jalil*, p. 362, refers to a single spring of Moses. However, the Qur'an relates that during the forty years that the Jews wandered in the desert, Moses at God's command took his rod and smote a rock, whereupon twelve streams of water gushed out in abundance (Qur'an, al-Baqarah: The Cow, 2:60, and al-'Araf: The Heights, 7:160). The springs were located in different regions of the Sinai, and the Jews were finally allowed to slake their thirst. The gushing of the springs was a sign of God's forgiveness and the end of their suffering. Throughout the Middle East, from the Sinai to Damascus, several holy sites associated with the prophet Moses can be found that are called Moses's springs.

8. This is a quotation from the Arabic translation by Salah Niazi of James Joyce's *Ulysses*.

9. Ibid.

10. Ibid.

11. "Babel" here refers to the ancient Babylon, situated along the Euphrates River. Ashur was the original capital of the Assyrian Empire and is now the location of a group of ruins on the right bank of the Tigris called Kalat Sherkat.

12. Eastern al-Quds, al-Quds al-sharqiyah, or East Jerusalem, was for many years the Arab section of Jerusalem. In 1967 Israel occupied East Jerusalem and effectively annexed the city in defiance of international law. Since then Israel has increased the Jewish Israeli presence in the city, weakened the Palestinian community by denying natives of the city the right to live there, and instituted other prohibitive policies. Israel has also impeded Palestinian urban development and has continually attempted to separate East Jerusalem from the rest of the Palestinian territories.

13. "Silent expulsion" refers to a tacit policy practiced by the Israeli government. As argued in an editorial in the Israeli newspaper *Haaretz*, the government applies "draconian regulations whose covert intent is to bring about the expulsion of as many Palestinians as possible from their home city": "The Silent Expulsion," *Haaretz*, June 22, 2010, available at: http://www.haaretz.com/the -silent-expulsion-1.297577.

14. The Holy Basin is the Israeli term for a geographical zone surrounding and including the historic

Old City; together, the basin and the walled enclosure contain the majority of sites holy to Islam, Judaism, and Christianity in the city. In recent times, the Holy Basin has become central to planning policy and political interests, for it is seen as the crux not only of how the city is contested but more generally of the Israeli-Palestinian conflict and the status of al-Quds/Jerusalem within the proposed two-state solution.

15. Silwan is a farming village southeast of the walls of the Old City that has been in existence since the medieval period. It lies in East al-Quds and was an exclusively Palestinian neighborhood from 1948 until the 1990s, when Israeli Jewish settler families began to move into the area.

16. Wadi Hilwa is an area of Silwan close to the Western Wall of the Old City.

17. Al-Bustan is a neighborhood in Wadi Hilwa.

18. There is no Sheikh Maddah neighborhood in any current map of al-Quds. It is possible that the poet is referring to the Sheikh Jarrah neighborhood in the city.

19. Wadi al-Rababa, also known as Hinnom Valley, is a picturesque stretch of land southwest of the Old City. It is the lowest point in the city. The Abu-Tur neighborhood lies to one side of the valley, and Silwan to the other. It holds great archeological interest for Zionists and contains graves dating back to the seventh century A.D.

20. "Solomon's stables," also known as the Marwani prayer hall, is an underground vaulted space now used as a Muslim prayer hall. The structure is believed to have been built by King Herod I as part of his extension of the platform of the Temple Mount, though some scholars suggest that the mosque was initially a water reservoir that had been built by the Roman emperor Hadrian in the second century, along with the stone wall currently surrounding al-Aqsa Mosque. During the Umayyad reign, this reservoir, along with the Dome of the Rock, was converted into a prayer hall by Caliph Abdul Malik bin Marwan. In 1099/492, Crusaders converted it into a stable for the infantry.

21. *Labaik! Labaik!* ("I am at your beck and call") is a devotional phrase in Arabic. It is a form of prayer recited continuously during pilgrimage to Mecca, directed to God. It can also be used as a response to an honorable and respected person; the companions of the Prophet Muhammad used the phrase when responding to him.

3. A Rope Between a Camel and a Tank

1. Al-Waqidi was a historian from Medina, born in the first half of the ninth/third century. He is the author of an early Islamic history and was of paramount importance for early Arabic historiography owing to the quantity and quality of the information which he passed on in literature, and for the nature of his methodology.

Al-Ya'qubi was an Arab historian and geographer in the second half of the ninth/third century. The principal importance of his historical work is that it is one of the earliest surviving examples of an Islamic "universal" history. It provides much insight and information on early Shiite attitudes, and contributed to the growth of historiography.

Al-Tabari (839–923/224/25–310) was a polymath. An expert in Islamic tradition and law, he is considered the greatest universal historian and Qur'an commentator of the first four centuries of Islam.

Ibn al-Batriq, also known as Eutychius of Alexandria, was the Melkite patriarch of Alexandria, appointed in 933/321 or 935/325 by the Abbasid caliph al-Qahir. He was the author of the historiographical treatise *Kitab Nazm al-Jawhar* (The String of Pearls), also known by its Latin title, *Eutychii Annales* (The Annals of Eutychius).

Al-Istukhri was an Arab geographer who lived in the first half of the tenth/fourth century. The geographic handbook *Kitab al-Maslik w'al Mamalik* (The Book of Roads and Kingdoms) is attributed to him. Little is known about his life.

Al-Massoudi (896–956/283–345) was an Arab historian who was born in Baghdad to a family which traced its genealogy to the companion (of the Prophet) Ibn Mas'ud. His principal work, *Muruj al-Dhahb wa Ma'adin al-Jawhir* (Meadows of God and Mines of Gems), cites 165 written sources, including, in addition to Arabic texts, translations of Plato, Aristotle, and Ptolemy.

Al-Maqdisi is the author of a historical encyclopedia, *Kitab al-Bd' w'al-Tarikh* (The Book of Beginnings and History), composed around 966/355, which covers everything from the creation of the world to the Umayyads and the Abbasids. Al-Maqdisi approaches his subject from a philosophical and critical point of view, and displays a good knowledge of ancient and alien regions.

Ibn 'Assakir was born in Damascus in 1105/499. His principal work, *Tarikh Madinat Dimashk* (History of the City of Damascus), is a biographical dictionary consisting of eighty volumes. After eulogizing the Prophet, the author enumerates in alphabetical order all the important people who dwelt in Damascus, either permanently or for a brief time. It is still consulted for the history of Damascus.

Osama ibn Munqid was by far the most famous of the Banu Munkidh tribe, which formed an emirate in northern Syria after capturing Shaizar and surrounding areas from the Byzantine Empire and ruling it for almost four decades (1081–1157/473–551). Ibn Munqid was esteemed in his own time as a poet and a man of letters and is known chiefly for his picturesque memoirs, *Kitab al-I'tibar* (Book of Instruction by Example). As was traditional in his family, he spent most of his life as a warrior and a politician.

Al-Imad al-Isbahani (b. 1125/519) was a historian, who came from a distinguished family in Isfahan but later studied in Baghdad. He was a close adviser to Saladin during his rule and military campaigns. The most remarkable of his works was a history of the conquest of al-Quds, *Al-Fath al-Qasi fi'l Fath al-Qudsi* (The Clear Enlightenment on the Jerusalemite Conquest).

Yaqout al-Hamawi (1179–1229/574–626) was born in Byzantine territory to non-Arab parents and became the slave of a man in Baghdad. After his emancipation, he traveled to many regions of the Arab world for trade and devoted much of his time to writing and learning. He is well known for works of geography, history, and poetry.

Ibn al-Athir (d. 1234/630) was a native of Jazirat ibn Umar, near Mosul, and is considered one of the most important Arab scholars and authors. He wrote a famous history, *Al-Kamil Fi'l-Tarikh* (The Complete History) among many other books.

Abu Sha'ma was a scholar of thirteenth/seventh-century Damascus, originally from al-Quds. He is best known for his histories and was one of the most important chroniclers of the Crusader and Ayyubid periods in Greater Syria.

Ibn al-'Ibri (1226–1286/623–684), known in the West as Bar Hebraeus, was a prelate of the Syrian Orthodox Church and the most prominent author of the Syriac Renaissance (eleventh to thirteenth/fifth to seventh century), a period in which Syriac Christian scholarship and literature flourished. He is best known to scholars of Islamic studies for his historical works, in which he combines Syriac, Arabic, and Persian sources.

Ibn Fadhl al-'Umri (b. 1301/700) was a distinguished author and administrator in the chancery of Cairo and Damascus. He is noted for his brilliance as a writer and his expertise in politics and administration.

Ibn Khaldoun (1332–1406/732–808) was born in Tunis and is considered one of the most significant Arab historians and historiographers of Arab-Muslim culture in the period of its decline. His main work, of universal value, is the *Muqaddima* (Prolegomena). *The Prolegomena* was intended as the introduction to his proposed world history, *Kitābu l-'ibari wa Dīwāni l-Mubtada' wal-Ḥabar fī ayāmi l-'arab wal-'ajam wal-barbar, waman 'Āsarahum min Dhawī sh-Shalṭāni l-Akbār* (Book of Lessons, Record of Beginnings, and Events in the History of the Arabs and Foreigners and Berbers and Their Powerful Contemporaries), but even in his lifetime it was regarded as an independent work. Ibn Khaldoun is considered a forerunner in the modern fields of demography and sociology.

Al-Maqrizi (1364–1442/765–845) was an Egyptian historian who spent many years teaching and writing in Mecca and Damascus, where he knew some of the greatest scholars of his time. Among his works were histories of the Fatimids, Ayyubids, and Mamluks.

Ibn Shahin (b. 1410/813), the son of a Mamluk, was born in Jerusalem and later lived in Cairo, where he had a distinguished administrative career under the Mamluks. He composed several major works, among them a book on Egyptian culture and society under the Mamluks, *Kashf al-mamlik fi bayan al-turuq wa al-masalik* (Revealing the Mamluks and Illuminating Their Ways and Means), as well as a book on the interpretation of dreams, *Al-Isharat fi 'ilm al-'ibarat* (The Signs in the Science of Explication).

Ibn Taghribirdi (1410–1470/813–874) was born in Cairo, the son of the commander-in-chief of the Egyptian army. He studied under many notable scholars and himself became the principal historian in Egypt. He wrote numerous biographies of sultans and other leaders, as well as works of poetry, history, and literature.

Shams-uldin Muhammad ibn Ahmad al-Suyuti (1410–1475/813–880) is the author of *Ithaf al-ikhsa bi-fad'il al-masjid al-aqsa* (Delighting the Gifted with Virtue of Masjid al-'Aqsa).

Majr al-Din al-Hanbali al-'Ulaymi (1456–1522/860–928) was an Arab historian who lived in al-Quds, where he served as *kadi kudat* (supreme judge). His principal work is a history in two volumes of al-Quds and al-Khalil/Hebron, titled *Al-Uns al-jalil bi-tarikh al-Quds wa-al-Khalil* (The Majestic Companion in the History of al-Quds and al-Khalil), the only extant history of al-Quds and some of the holy places of Palestine.

2. This is a hadith found in al-'Ulaymi, *Al-Uns al-jalil*, p. 360.

3. Part of hadith 19382 in the *Sunan al-Bayhaqi al-Kubra*, vol. 9, p. 534. *Sunan al-Bayhaqi al-Kubra* (Al-Bayhaqi's Enlarged Collection) is a multivolume collection of hadiths edited and catalogued by Ahmad ibn al-Hussein ibn Ali ibn Musa al-Khorasani al-Bayhaqi (994–1065/384–458).

4. Ibid.

4. A Bridge to Job

1. The Moroccan Quarter was a 770-year-old neighborhood in the southeast corner of the Old City. It was founded by a son of Saladin in the late twelfth century. The quarter was razed by Israeli forces after the Six-Day War in order to broaden the narrow alley leading to the Western Wall to make it more accessible for Jewish worshippers seeking to pray there.

The "woman Europe was named after" is Europa, who in Greek mythology was carried off and raped by Zeus in the form of a bull. Of Phoenician origin, she was the mother of King Minos of Crete, and the sister of Cadmus, who brought the alphabet to mainland Greece.

2. "Allah is the Light of the heavens and the earth. The Parable of His Light is as if there were a Niche and within it a Lamp: the Lamp enclosed in Glass: the glass as it were a brilliant star: Lit from a blessed Tree, an Olive, neither of the east nor of the west, whose oil is well-nigh luminous, though fire scarce touched it: Light upon Light! Allah doth guide whom He will to His Light: Allah doth set forth Parables for men: and Allah doth know all things" (Qur'an, al-Nur: The Light, 24:35).

3. In the book of Job (1:1-20) Satan is allowed to afflict Job to test his faith. He causes the Sabeans and Chaldeans to steal Job's oxen, asses, and camels and kill his servants. A fire burns up the

sheep and the shepherds, and a great wind from the wilderness tears down the house where Job's sons and daughters are feasting and kills them. The reference in this passage is what is left after Job's affliction begins: such destruction is a kind of malevolent feast.

4. Averroës (1126–1198/520–594) is the Latinized name of Ibn Rushd ('Abu al-Walid Muhammad ibn Ahmad ibn Rushd), a Spanish Arab philosopher. Born in Cordova, he studied law and medicine in his native town, and later became a *kadi*, judge. He wrote many important commentaries and books on philosophy including responses to the works of philosophers such as imam Ghazali and al-Farabi. Averroës was an influential proponent of rationality in Arabic and Islamic thought. As such he stands for rationality here, while the apple, as the symbol of the human fall from paradise, stands for the irrational in all the monotheistic traditions, Islam among them. The comparison makes an ironic statement on the way the rational and the irrational coexist in disharmony in Islamic societies now.

Averroës is also famous as a commentator on Aristotle, who also used the apple as a metaphor in one of his discourses. In his translation and commentary on Aristotle, written for Caliph Almohad Abu Yaqub Yusuf, Averroës argues that the power to judge "is divisible according to being and indivisible according to place and number. Perhaps what judges different things and contraries is divisible according to being and form, but indivisible according to subject and according to matter, as we say about the apple that it is indivisible in subject and divisible according to different kinds of being in it, namely, color, smell, and flavor" (quoted in Averroës, *Long Commentary on the De Anima of Aristotle*, trans. Richard C. Taylor [New Haven: Yale University Press, 2011]).

5. This is a reference to a well-known Arab proverb: "Give a bow to the maker of bows." The implication is that things are resolved only by the person who has the most practical knowledge about a given problem. Here the mob has come to the maker of bows to see if he is indeed a maker, demanding that he show proof.

6. A description of the Day of Judgment in the Qur'an. "When the earth is shaken to her (utmost) convulsion" (al-Zalzala: The Earthquake, 99:1).

7. Maimonides, in his *Guide of the Perplexed*, explains that when a saying has two meanings "the external meaning ought to be as beautiful as silver, while its internal meaning ought to be more beautiful than the external one . . . as happens in the case of an apple of gold overlaid with silver filigree-work having very small holes. When looked at from a distance or with imperfect attention, it is deemed to be an apple of silver; but when a keen-sighted observer looks at it with full attention, its interior becomes clear to him and he knows that it is of gold. The parables of the prophets, peace be upon them, are similar. Their external meaning contains wisdom that is useful in many respects, among which is welfare of human societies. . . . Their internal meaning, on the other hand, contains wisdom that is useful for beliefs concerned with truth as it is" (Moses Mai-

monides, *The Guide of the Perplexed*, vol. 1, trans. Shlomo Pines [Chicago: University of Chicago Press, 2010]).

8. The poet here is playing on the Arabic translation of the word *Mediterranean, al-mutawasit,* "middle" or "medium"; *tawasut* refers to fairness, mediation, and moderation. The Mediterranean is a midland sea, but it lacks moderation and fairness.

9. *Sama'* is the Arabic word for sky. I inserted it here so that the letters of the Arabic alphabet that make up the word would make sense as they are listed and commented on in the poem.

10. Leviticus 25:44–46 (New American Standard Bible, 1977).

11. Habakkuk 2:12. Adonis quotes from the Arabic translation of the Good News Bible, available at the Arab Church website, http://www.arabchurch.com/ArabicBible/gna/Habakkuk/2. In the New International Version, this passage reads, "Woe to him who builds a city with bloodshed and establishes a town by injustice!" Although most of the Arabic translations I reviewed make a distinction between a city, which is established on bloodshed, and a town, established on injustice, the translation the poet used does not. In attributing both violations to Jerusalem, the poet offers a double indictment of the city.

5. Dissection

1. The story of Solomon and the hoopoe is found in the Qur'an (al-Naml: The Ant, 27:20–44): "And he took a muster of the Birds; and he said: 'Why is it I see not the Hoopoe? Or is he among the absentees? I will certainly punish him with a severe penalty, or execute him, unless he bring me a clear reason (for absence).' But the Hoopoe tarried not far: he (came up and) said: 'I have compassed (territory) which thou hast not compassed, and I have come to thee from Saba with tidings true'" (20–22). At this time, the kingdom of Sheba did not worship one god, but at the end of the tale, the queen, Bilqis, and all her people willingly accept the religion of Solomon. Legend has it that Solomon and Bilqis were married.

2. Abdul Malik ibn Marwan, the fifth caliph of the Umayyad line, reigned 685–705/65–86 and was succeeded by his eldest son, al-Walid. Abdul Malik built the Dome of the Rock in the Old City.

3. Buraq Square is the open area near the Buraq Wall (also known as the Western Wall), which is located in the Old City. It is a relatively small western segment of the wall surrounding the area called the Temple Mount by Jews, Christians, and most Westerners and al-Haram al-Sharif (The Noble Sanctuary) by Muslims. It is one of the oldest and most important religious sites in the Old City. The present site is dominated by three monumental structures: the al-Aqsa Mosque, the Dome of the Rock, and the Dome of the Chain. Al-Buraq is the flying steed of the prophets, upon which the Prophet Muhammad rode on his nighttime journey (Isra) from Mecca to al-Quds.

4. "The Messenger has believed in what was revealed to him from his Lord, and [so have] the be-

lievers. All of them have believed in Allah and His angels and His books and His messengers, [saying,] 'We make no distinction between any of His messengers.' And they say, 'We hear and we obey. [We seek] Your forgiveness, our Lord, and to You is the [final] destination'" (Qur'an, al-Baqarah: The Cow, 2:285).

5. Al-Nafaq al-Gharbi (Western Wall Tunnel) is an underground tunnel running the full length of the Western Wall. The tunnel is adjacent to the wall and located under the buildings of the Old City. 'Ain Silwan is the famed spring from which the neighborhood of Silwan takes its name.

6. The image of eavesdropping, or "stealing" a hearing—listening in to hear what one is not allowed to hear—whereby demons and jinn try to steal the revelations of prophets or angels, is found in the Qur'an: "It is We Who have set out the zodiacal signs in the heavens, and made them fair-seeming to (all) beholders; And (moreover) We have guarded them from every evil spirit accursed: But any that gains a hearing by stealth, is pursued by a flaming fire, bright (to see)" (Hijr: The Rocky Tract, 15:16–18).

7. The Synagogue of Ohel Yitchak is a Hungarian synagogue located in the Muslim Quarter of the Old City. It was built in the 1870s by Kolel Shomrei HaChomos, an organization of Hungarian Jews, but was abandoned after rioting in 1938. Although the building was destroyed after 1948, it has recently been acquired by a religious Zionist group for refurbishment.

8. The Hammam al-'Ain is one of the two oldest public baths in the Old City; the other is the Hammam al-Shifa. Both were built under Roman rule and are located in the Muslim Quarter.

9. Tankiz Khan was an inn for travelers built by Sayf al-Din Tankiz, the governor of Damascus from 1312 to 1340/711 to 740. It was still functioning in the sixteenth century. It is located in Jaljulia, an Arab town in the state of Israel near Kfar Saba.

10. Beit Hatsalam and Beit Sharon were built by Israelis aiming to settle Jews in the Muslim Quarter of the Old City. Beit Hatsalam (the Photographer's House) now houses several Jewish families. Beit Sharon is a large house acquired by the late Israeli prime minister Ariel Sharon as part of his plan to assert Israel's intention to annex the whole city. He never spent any time there.

11. Damascus Gate is one of the main entrances to the Old City. It is located on the northwest side where the highway leads out to Nablus, and from there, in times past, went on to Damascus.

Al-Wad Street is a road lined with ancient shops in the Old City. It is an important historical and cultural site and was one of the main places of trade for merchants of ancient times.

The Cardo was a double-columned main thoroughfare in al-Quds/Jerusalem built by the Romans as part of their reconstruction of the city in the second century A.D. The Cardo starts at Damascus Gate in the north, traversing the city southward up to the Jewish Quarter gate.

Documenas Maximus in Roman urban planning is an east-west street that intersects with the Cardo and served as a secondary main street of al-Quds/Jerusalem.

Byzantium, the Ummayads, the Abbasids, the Crusaders, the Ayyubites, the Mamluks, and the British are all kingdoms, dynasties, or peoples that ruled al-Quds/Jerusalem from the collapse of the Roman Empire to the creation of the state of Israel in 1948/1367.

12. Solomon's Cave, also known as Solomon's quarries, is a five-acre underground limestone quarry that runs the length of five city blocks under the Muslim Quarter of the Old City.

13. The Land of Sabra is an area adjacent to Harat al-Sharaf (Lane of Honor), located in the Jewish Quarter of the Old City. It is a focus of Jewish settlers who after seizing it are using it to expand their existing settlements by means of excavations and construction.

The "earth's anguish" is *'adhab al-ardh*; it could also be a reference to *'adhab al-qabr* (the punishment of the grave). A common belief among Muslims, supported by a saying of the Prophet Muhammad, holds that infidels will be punished in their graves from the time of their death to the Day of Judgment.

14. The Souk al-Khawajat is among the three major markets located within the walls of the Old City; the other two are the markets of Hamieen and Attareen. The Souk al-Khawajat is famous for shops that sell and tailor traditional woven clothing. Due to an earthquake in A.D. 1927, the northern section of the souk was damaged and never reconstructed. The back of the market is set against the Western Wall of the Sultan Khan.

15. The northeastern tower in the al-Quds/Jerusalem city wall is known as Burj al-Laqlaq (Stork Tower).

16. In medieval Muslim tradition, the spring of Silwan, south of the village, was among the four most sacred water sources in the world. The others were Zamzam in Mecca, the spring of Falus in Beisan, and the spring of Baqar in Acre. The word *'ain* in Arabic means both "eye" and "spring," as in hot spring. Adonis plays on the dual meaning of the word, and in my translation I tried to convey that double meaning by including both words.

17. The Land of Sayyam is a plot of land in al-Quds/Jerusalem owned by the Sayyam family that Israeli authorities are attempting to expropriate for archaeological purposes. The word *Sayyam* in Arabic means "fasting." Here Adonis is playing on the double meaning of the family name in addressing the horizon.

18. Wadi Hilwa, the area of Silwan close to the Western Wall of the Old City, and its neighborhood of al-Bustan, have been a focus of Jewish settlement.

19. Talat al-Dhuhour/City of David is a hill near the Silwan spring that was the first area inhabited in al-Quds/Jerusalem and is considered the seed of the city. Solomon later chose it as his capital. The Israeli government is conducting digs and constructing tunnels in the area as a first step toward creating Jewish settlements in this part of the Arab Quarter. They have renamed the city City of David (Talat al-Dhuhour).

20. 'Ain Um-al-Darj Spring, also known as the Fountain of the Virgin, is located in the Kidron Valley and was one of the essential springs for human settlement in ancient al-Quds/Jerusalem, providing both drinking water and water for irrigating farmlands and vegetable gardens for the settlements.

21. Chain Street/Silsila runs perpendicular to the Souk al-Attarin (Cardo market) in the Old City, going gently downhill to the Gate of the Chain, the most important entrance to the Haram al-Sharif (Temple Mount). This was the great residential street of medieval Islamic al-Quds. It starts out as a typical market passageway, but as it nears the Haram, it is characterized by monumental, richly ornamented doorways of Mamluk-period mansions and buildings decorated with carved stonework in "stalactite" patterns over the entryways. Many of these are hidden behind shop signs, however, and like much of the Old City, the neighborhood is today overcrowded. It has not benefited from preservation and renovation programs.

22. Via Dolorosa, the "Way of Sorrows," is the street within the Old City that Christians believe was the path walked by Jesus on the way to his crucifixion. The winding route from the Antonia Fortress west to the Church of the Holy Sepulchre is a celebrated place of Christian pilgrimage.

6. Afflictions

1. Matthew 21 contains a prophecy that Jesus will come to Jerusalem on a donkey with a foal. "Say to Daughter Zion, 'See, your king comes to you, gentle and riding on a donkey, and on a colt, the foal of a donkey'" (New International Version).

2. The reference here is to Hagar, wife or concubine of Ibrahim (Abraham) and mother of Ismail (Ishmael). The Arabs and Muslims consider themselves descendants of Ismail, hence, the concubine's children.

3. Salome in the New Testament is the daughter of Herod II and Herodias. She is responsible for the execution of John the Baptist, who criticized her mother's divorce from her first husband. Some Greek texts show that Salome may have also been called Herodias like her mother. The poet here engages in wordplay with "Herodia" by turning it into "Hiroshima." I try to replicate the wordplay by also adding the clarification regarding the names of Salome/Herodia.

4. The Qur'an refers to al-riyah al-lawaqih, winds that fertilize or are fertilized. "And We send the fecundating winds, then cause the rain to descend from the sky, therewith providing you with water (in abundance), though ye are not the guardians of its stores"(Hijr: The Rocky Tract, 15:22). The quotation is a hadith found in al-Maqdisi, *Muthir al-gharam*, and al-Suyuti, *Ithaf al-ikhsa bi-fad'il al-masjid al-aqsa*, 1/155, quoted in al-'Ulaymi, *Al-Uns al-jalil*, p. 352.

5. "Omega" is a reference to Revelation 22:13: "I am Alpha and Omega, the First and the Last, the

Beginning and the End" (New International Version). The poet here imagines a Palestinian-Jewish end, an Omega to the conflict. The poet's vision of the fusion of the two peoples is ironic. In the last line of the passage the poet refers to the veil being the fatwa of the hour, which imagines the fundamentalist forces of Judaism, Christianity, and Islam becoming joined by their desire to cover and restrict women's bodies, as they concur on many of their teachings.

6. The poet uses the word *hawdh*, which means both "basin" and "uterus." I indicate both meanings to convey this duality.

7. Tempted by Nothing

1. The Arabic phrase *malik al-sina'at*, "king of trades," is commonly used in advertisements. Here the reference is to the person or entity with the greatest power or hegemony, probably God.

8. Tempted by Everything

1. About 10,000 square feet.

2. This quotation is a hadith found in al-Suyuti, *Ithaf al-ikhsa bi-fad'il al-masjid al-aqsa*, 1/130, quoted in al-'Ulaymi, *Al-Uns al-jalil*, p. 357.

3. This quotation is a hadith found in al-Maqdisi, *Muthir al-gharam*, quoted in al-'Ulaymi, *Al-Uns al-jalil*, p. 353.

4. The poet uses the words *haj* and *'umra*, describing the two kinds of pilgrimages that Muslims make to Mecca and Medina. The haj pilgrimage is one of the five pillars of Islam, and it must be performed during the Islamic month of Dhi al-Hijja, the last month in the Hijri calendar and concluding on the tenth day of that month, which is the Feast of Sacrifice, or Eid al-Adha. All Muslims are required to perform this ritual once in a lifetime if they are able. Muslims may also perform another kind of pilgrimage called the 'umra. This is not a required ritual and may be performed at any time of the year. The poet mentions both rituals, but to avoid confusion I have referred to pilgrimage in general. Masjid al-Haram is the grand mosque of Mecca, the holiest site of Islam. The entire quotation is a hadith found in al-Maqdisi, *Muthir al-gharam*, and al-Suyuti, *Ithaf al-ikhsa bi-fad'il al-masjid al-aqsa*, 1/151, quoted in al-'Ulaymi, *Al-Uns al-jalil*, p. 352.

Part II. Images

1. The line here borrows a phrase from the Qur'an: "Have We not expanded thee thy breast?—And removed from thee thy burden?" (al-Sharh: Solace, 94:1–2).

2. The poet here refers to the seduction scene in the story of Yusuf (Joseph) in the Qur'an, Yusuf:

Joseph, 12:23: "And she, in whose house he was, sought to seduce him. She closed the doors and said, 'Come, take what is yours!' He said, '[I seek] the refuge of Allah. Indeed, he is my master, who has made good my residence. Indeed, wrongdoers will not succeed'" (translation mine). See also Genesis 39:12.

3. The Arab world is often described as the land between the Arabian/Persian Gulf and the Atlantic Ocean.

4. "The Day that We roll up the heavens like a scroll rolled up for books . . . even as We produced the first creation, so shall We produce a new one: a promise We have undertaken: truly shall We fulfil it" (Qur'an, al-Anbiyaa: The Prophets, 21:104).

5. The poet is using the Arabic preposition *bi*, which like the French *de* has different layers of meaning. Here the poet plays with the Arabic (also biblical commandment's) phrase "al-'ain bil-'ain, wa al-sin bil-sin" or "an eye for an eye and a tooth for a tooth." However, the Arabic *bi* can mean both "for" and "with." In the translation, I tried to capture the doubleness the poet conveys by translating the first as "for" and the second as "with."

6. The poet here uses the Arabic phrase "ma malakat aimanukum," which literally means "what you possess in your hands," but usually refers to the slaves and concubines of a believer. Several verses in the Qur'an and sayings by the Prophet Muhammad command the believer to be generous and merciful to those under his command.

7. According to Numbers 19:1–10 the ashes of an unblemished red heifer that has never been yoked are a requirement for purifying those who come in contact with the dead and temples. Some Jews and Christians (for whom the heifer is a symbol of Christ) believe that the emergence of a red heifer is a precondition to the building of the third temple (which is to be built on the site of the Haram al-Sharif). As such it is seen as a signal for the end times, as stated in Ezekiel 41–45, and Matthew 24. In modern times continual efforts have been made to locate such a heifer, but none has been found that meets the conditions stipulated by Jewish law. Some Jewish and Christian Zionist groups have attempted to use modern technology to produce a red heifer.

8. The Qur'an reports on an invasion of the city of Mecca by an Abyssinian army led by King Abraha (a Christian ruler of Yemen) accompanied by a troop of elephants. God saved the Meccans by sending a swarm of birds that pelted the invaders with clay stones and drove them away. "Seest thou not how thy Lord dealt with the People of the Elephant? Did He not make their treacherous plan go astray? And He sent against them Flights of Birds [*ababil*]. Striking them with stones of baked clay. Then did He make them like an empty field of stalks and straw, (of which the corn) has been eaten up" (Qur'an, al-Feel: The Elephant, 105:1–5). The occasion became marked as the year of the elephant and is believed to be the year the Prophet Muhammad was born.

ACKNOWLEDGMENTS

The translator and author wish to thank the following journals: *Banipal: A Journal of Modern Arabic Literature, Image Journal, The Colorado Review,* and *The Kenyon Review Online* for publishing extracts from the poem.

We are grateful to Anton Shammas and Bassam Frangieh for their support of the project.

We are also immensely thankful to Wijdan al-Sayegh for her review of the translation's accuracy, and to Ali Zindah for his assistance with assembling the numerous notes that were required for the translation.

Gratitude and boundless appreciation also go to Susan Laity at Yale University Press for her meticulous work on the text and the notes.

ADONIS was born Ali Ahmad Sa'id in western Syria in 1930. He is heralded as the leader of the modernist movement in Arabic literature. His work includes over fifty books of poetry, criticism, and translation. In 2011, he won the Goethe Prize.

KHALED MATTAWA is the author of four books of poetry and the translator of nine volumes of contemporary Arabic poetry. A MacArthur Foundation Fellow, Mattawa is professor of English and Creative Writing at the University of Michigan.